UNDERSTANDING AMERICAN DEMOCRACY
RULE BY THE PEOPLE

by Janie Havemeyer

San Diego, CA

BrightPoint Press

© 2024 BrightPoint Press
an imprint of ReferencePoint Press, Inc.
Printed in the United States

For more information, contact:
BrightPoint Press
PO Box 27779
San Diego, CA 92198
www.BrightPointPress.com

ALL RIGHTS RESERVED.

No part of this work covered by the copyright hereon may be reproduced or used in any form or by any means—graphic, electronic, or mechanical, including photocopying, recording, taping, web distribution, or information storage retrieval systems—without the written permission of the publisher.

LIBRARY OF CONGRESS CATALOGING-IN-PUBLICATION DATA

Names: Havemeyer, Janie, author.
Title: Rule by the people / by Janie Havemeyer.
Description: San Diego, CA: BrightPoint Press, 2024. | Series: Understanding American democracy | Includes bibliographical references and index. | Audience: Ages 13 | Audience: Grades 7-9
Identifiers: LCCN 2023012484 (print) | LCCN 2023012485 (eBook) | ISBN 9781678206987 (hardcover) | ISBN 9781678206994 (eBook)
Subjects: LCSH: Political participation--United States--Juvenile literature. | Representative government and representation--United States--Juvenile literature. | United States--Politics and government--Juvenile literature.
Classification: LCC JK1764 .H394 2024 (print) | LCC JK1764 (eBook) | DDC 323/.0420973--dc23/eng/20230404
LC record available at https://lccn.loc.gov/2023012484
LC eBook record available at https://lccn.loc.gov/2023012485

CONTENTS

AT A GLANCE	4
INTRODUCTION YOUR VOTE IS YOUR VOICE	6
CHAPTER ONE THE ORIGINS OF US DEMOCRACY	12
CHAPTER TWO THE ROLE OF CITIZENS	22
CHAPTER THREE PARTICIPATING IN GOVERNMENT	28
CHAPTER FOUR THE FUTURE OF DEMOCRACY	46
Glossary	58
Source Notes	59
For Further Research	60
Index	62
Image Credits	63
About the Author	64

AT A GLANCE

- Democracy is a form of government where the people rule.

- The US Constitution was written in 1787. This document explains the structures and processes of American democracy.

- Many changes have been made to the Constitution since it was first written. These changes are called amendments.

- Citizens in a democracy choose leaders by voting in elections. US citizens eighteen years or older have the right to vote.

- Not all citizens have always been able to vote in US elections. In 1787, only white men who owned property could vote. Black Americans, women, and Native Americans had to fight for the right to vote.

- Technology makes it easier to take part in democracy. It helps voters get information about where and how to vote. Candidates also use technology to reach out to voters.

- Citizens can participate in democracy by speaking up about important issues. They can get involved by running for office or leading protests.

- Some modern voting laws, such as voter identification requirements, make it harder for some Americans to vote.

INTRODUCTION

YOUR VOTE IS YOUR VOICE

In 1974, eighteen-year-old Iris Galvan was a student in Texas. She was part of United Youth. This group worked on getting Mexican Americans to vote. Volunteers spoke with people in the Mexican community. They helped them understand how US politics worked. They informed them about **candidates** running for office.

Iris watched an old man pushing a food cart up the street. She smiled at him. "Have you ever thought about voting?" she asked. "You have a right to vote. You are a

Volunteers can make a difference by registering voters. They can help people fill out voter registration forms.

Poll workers may greet voters, answer questions, and explain how to mark ballots correctly.

citizen of this country." The man shrugged. Spanish was his first language. "I don't speak very good English," he said.[1] Iris nodded. She understood.

Iris came from a family of farm workers. Her grandparents had crossed the Mexican border in 1908. Iris's grandmother had told her, "You are very smart. You can be . . . whatever you want to be."[2] As Iris got older, she learned to speak up. She voted in her first **election**. She chose candidates on the **ballot** who would help her community.

Iris and other volunteers walked through their neighborhoods. They encouraged people to vote. They explained how Spanish-speaking voters could get help at the **polls**.

It is every US citizen's duty to elect leaders. By voting, they have a say in who runs the country. Iris educated voters about different candidates. She helped them understand why voting mattered.

AMERICAN DEMOCRACY

Democracy is the system of government in the United States. The United States was formed in 1776. The country's founders met in 1787 to decide how the government would work. They made it a representative democracy. This means citizens vote for officials to run the government. These leaders represent the people who elect them. The US Constitution explains how democracy works. It describes the three

Citizens can create change by protesting. In 2017, thousands of people participated in the Women's March in Washington, DC.

branches of government and their powers. It also explains the rights of citizens.

A democracy works best when everyone gets involved. One way to get involved is by voting. Citizens can also speak up and protest. In a democracy, ordinary citizens have the power to create change.

1
THE ORIGINS OF US DEMOCRACY

Democracy comes from the Greek word *demokratia*. *Demo* means "the people." *Kratos* means "power." The idea of democracy began in Greece more than 2,000 years ago. Cleisthenes was a Greek leader. He came up with a government system in which the people ruled.

Democracy in ancient Greece was different from democracy in the United States. It was a direct democracy. This means citizens vote directly for the laws they follow. They are not represented by elected officials.

Cleisthenes was from Athens, which is the capital city of modern Greece. Athens is often considered the birthplace of democracy.

Early settlers in North America had a similar type of democracy. The Pilgrims were a group of settlers from England. England was ruled by a king. The Pilgrims left England and set up a colony in North America. In 1620, they created the Mayflower Compact. This was a set of laws that the Pilgrims used to rule themselves in the colony. The Mayflower Compact followed the Greek idea of direct democracy. The Pilgrims made laws and agreed to follow them. The United States was formed 156 years later. It would be founded on the idea of rule by the people.

In 1773, some colonists protested tea taxes by boarding British ships and throwing cases of tea into Boston Harbor.

THE DECLARATION OF INDEPENDENCE

By the 1700s, there were thirteen colonies in North America. These colonies were ruled by England. People who lived in the colonies were called colonists. They grew

Fifty-six delegates signed the Declaration of Independence.

tired of being ruled by England. England was governed by a king and Parliament, which was an assembly of men. They made decisions about the colonies, such as requiring colonists to pay taxes to the king. The colonists were angry that no one represented them in Parliament. They wanted a say in how they were governed.

Tensions between England and the colonies led to the Revolutionary War (1775–1783). The colonists fought to win independence from England. In 1776, revolution leaders wrote the Declaration of Independence. This document announced that the colonists would form a new nation called the United States of America.

The declaration said that a government gets its power from its people. This means people have the power to choose their leaders. They shape the laws that govern them. Thomas Jefferson helped write the Declaration of Independence. He said the strongest government is one "of which every man feels himself a part."[3] The ideas in the Declaration of Independence are still important today.

THE US CONSTITUTION

The thirteen colonies became the first US states. At first, each state governed

APPROVING THE CONSTITUTION

Each state had a meeting to approve the Constitution. Nine out of thirteen states had to accept the document for it to become law. New Hampshire was the ninth state to approve the document. In 1789, the Constitution was **ratified**.

itself. But by 1787, America needed a more powerful central government. This would protect all citizens' rights and freedoms. Representatives from each state met in Philadelphia to create the US Constitution.

This document explains how the US government works. It created three branches of government. One is the legislative branch, or Congress. It writes bills that might become laws. The judicial branch is the courts. The courts settle disputes and make sure people follow laws. The executive branch includes the president. He or she signs or rejects bills. Each branch has power. But the nation's founders made sure that no branch could become more powerful than the others.

The Constitution begins with the words, "We the People of the United States, in Order to form a more perfect Union . . . do ordain and establish this Constitution."[4] This means the Constitution is a document for the people. The government serves the people. It does not rule over them. Citizens rule themselves. This was a big change from being ruled by a king. The phrase *We the People* was meant to include all citizens. But when the Constitution was written, not everyone living in the country had citizenship. Only white men who owned property were citizens.

The first US president was George Washington. He was a Revolutionary War leader. He said the new government was an experiment "entrusted to the hands of the American people."[5] It was up to the people to rule the new nation wisely.

CELEBRATING CITIZENS

September 17 is Constitution and Citizenship Day. It was created by Congress in 1952. It is a day to celebrate the signing of the Constitution. It is also a day to honor US citizens and remember their rights.

2

THE ROLE OF CITIZENS

In the United States, ordinary citizens choose government leaders. They do this by voting in elections. Elections are free and fair. Voters can vote freely for candidates they want. No one can force them to vote for candidates they do not want. In a fair election, all voters have the opportunity to vote. All votes are counted.

Citizens ages eighteen and older can vote. The Constitution says the government gets its power from the people. The people

Voters are assigned to polling places based on where they live. Polling places are often community buildings such as schools.

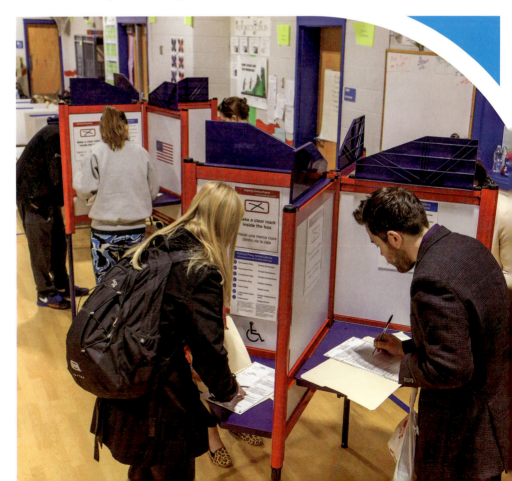

make decisions by voting. US citizens are not required to vote. But voting is considered the duty of all citizens. For a democracy to work, citizens must vote.

CITIZENS' RIGHTS

The Constitution also protects people's rights, or freedoms. One section of the Constitution is the Bill of Rights. It lists the rights of US citizens.

FIRST PRESIDENTIAL ELECTION

The first US presidential election was on February 4, 1789. George Washington was elected. He took office on April 30. The ceremony was held in New York City. Washington was elected president two times.

The process of becoming a US citizen is called naturalization. People become citizens at a naturalization ceremony.

Citizens are people born in the United States. People are also citizens if they are born overseas but their parents are citizens. People from other countries can become US citizens too. To do so, they must pass exams in English and promise to be loyal.

All US citizens must follow rules, such as obeying laws and paying taxes. These laws help the government keep order and protect citizens. Citizens also have rights. One right is to vote for government leaders.

BECOMING A CITIZEN

Susana Westbrook was born in Mexico. She lived in the United States for many years with her husband, who was a US citizen. Susana decided to become a citizen too. She had to pass exams with questions about US history. Susana said becoming a citizen was one of the biggest accomplishments of her life. "It all meant so much to me," she said.

Quoted in "Welcome in the Workplace: CLINIC Staff Share Stories of Naturalization," CLINIC, *September 8, 2022. www.cliniclegal.org.*

Citizens can also get involved by participating in a candidate's campaign. To run for government positions, people need support and funding. Citizens can make phone calls to gain support for a candidate. They might raise money for candidates too.

Citizens can also gather and protest for a common cause. When many citizens speak up, leaders pay attention. Barack Obama was the forty-fourth US president. He spoke about the power of ordinary people in a democracy. He said, "The most important title is not 'president' or 'prime minister'; the most important title is 'citizen.'"[6]

3

PARTICIPATING IN GOVERNMENT

Citizens can participate in government in many ways. One way is by running for office. People can serve their communities by becoming elected officials. Elected officials may serve cities, towns, states, or the entire nation. They serve every citizen, not just the people who voted for them.

Voting is another way to participate. In 2021, Joe Biden became the forty-sixth US president. In 2022, he spoke about protecting voting rights. He said, "We want Americans to vote. We want every

People can run for positions such as governor, senator, mayor, or city council member.

American's voice to be heard."[7] But not everyone has always been able to vote. Over time, changes have been made to the Constitution. These are called **amendments**. By 2023, there had been twenty-seven amendments to the Constitution.

THE FOURTEENTH AND FIFTEENTH AMENDMENTS

In 1789, only white male property owners were able to vote. Black people were not considered citizens. Hundreds of thousands of them were enslaved by white colonists.

Many Black men fought for the Union during the Civil War. Most of them had been formerly enslaved.

Slavery was a big business in the southern states. The first enslaved Black people were brought to Virginia in 1619. In the 1700s, white people brought more enslaved people to America to work on farms. There were many large farms in the southern states. Farmers forced enslaved people to harvest crops on these farms.

In 1860, Abraham Lincoln ran for president. He planned to stop slavery from spreading. When Lincoln became president,

THE GETTYSBURG ADDRESS

In 1863, a major Civil War battle took place at Gettysburg, Pennsylvania. Union and Confederate soldiers fought for three days. The Union won the battle. Afterward, President Lincoln gave a speech. It was called the Gettysburg Address. He said the Union was fighting to protect "government of the people, by the people, for the people."

Quoted in "The Gettysburg Address, 1863," Gilder Lehrman Institute of American History, n.d. www.gilderlehrman.org.

many southern states were unhappy. They depended on enslaved people to harvest their crops. Eleven southern states broke away from the United States and made their own government. They called it the Confederacy. The northern states were called the Union. The southern and northern states disagreed about slavery. This led to the American Civil War (1861–1865).

    The Union won the Civil War. After the war, slavery ended. Black men demanded the right to vote. Over 200,000 Black men fought for their country in the war. They wanted to take part in running it.

Two amendments helped Black men win the right to vote.

In 1868, the Fourteenth Amendment was passed. It said all people born in the United States were citizens. This meant formerly enslaved people were now citizens. It also said that all men over twenty-one could vote. But white people tried to prevent Black men from voting because of their race.

In 1870, the Fifteenth Amendment was passed. It said the right to vote could not be denied because of a person's race or color. It also said formerly enslaved people could vote. This amendment gave voting

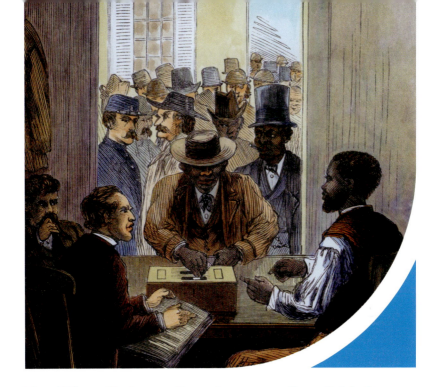

The Fifteenth Amendment gave voting rights to Black men in all US states.

rights to Black men. But many southern states passed laws to prevent Black citizens from voting. Some states required citizens to pay poll taxes. Many Black people could not afford to pay these taxes. Some states also required citizens to prove they could read. Formerly enslaved people had not

Suffragists organized protests, marches, parades, and other demonstrations to fight for the vote.

had the chance to go to school. Many of them couldn't read. Another rule was the grandfather clause. It said that reading tests and other voting rules did not apply to poor whites. They could vote if their grandfathers had voted before the Civil War. These laws made it hard for Black citizens to vote.

THE NINETEENTH AMENDMENT

Before 1920, women could not vote in **federal** elections. After the Civil War, many women began fighting for voting rights. **Suffragists** such as Elizabeth Cady Stanton and Susan B. Anthony helped lead the fight for women's suffrage. In 1869, they founded the National Woman Suffrage Association (NWSA). In 1890, NWSA merged with another group to form the National American Woman Suffrage

Suffragists from a group called the National Woman's Party protested outside the White House. They were known as the Silent Sentinels.

Association (NAWSA). NAWSA helped local and state groups fight for the right to vote.

By the early 1900s, many suffragists marched in parades. Some protested in front of the White House. They carried signs. One sign asked the president how long women had to wait for liberty. Some of the protesters were arrested.

In 1919, twenty-six suffragists went on a train tour called the Prison Special. They had all been imprisoned for their suffrage work. The women visited states where they needed support. They shared stories about being mistreated in prison. They helped more people understand why women should have voting rights. In 1920, the Nineteenth Amendment was passed. This gave women the right to vote.

VOTING RIGHTS ACT OF 1965

The Fifteenth and Nineteenth Amendments helped Black citizens and women win the vote. But it was still difficult for Black citizens to vote. Some states passed new laws that kept them from voting.

Over the next four decades, Black citizens fought for full voting rights. Black voters were often threatened and treated badly at the polls. If Black citizens could not vote, they could not be fairly represented. They could not improve their communities.

In 1965, the Voting Rights Act was passed. This banned reading tests and other voting practices that made it difficult for Black people to vote. The law was aimed at southern states, which had barred many

After the Voting Rights Act of 1965, more Black citizens registered to vote.

Black citizens from voting. President Lyndon Johnson signed the act into law. He said that it was wrong to deny any Americans the right to vote. After the act, the number of Black voters grew significantly. By the late 1960s, there were more than a million new Black voters.

HOLDING PUBLIC OFFICE

In the United States, many people can run for office. But there are rules about who can run for office. These rules differ from state to state. Some rules say candidates must live in the same place as the people they represent. Candidates must have lived in a place for a certain amount of time. For some positions, there are rules about how old candidates must be. For example, candidates may run for the House of Representatives. This is part of Congress. Its members are known as congresspeople. They must be at least

Members of Congress attend meetings at the US Capitol in Washington, DC.

twenty-five years old. And they must have been citizens for seven years or more.

To run for president, a person must be at least thirty-five years old. The person must have been born a US citizen. He or she must also have lived in the United States for at least fourteen years.

Some elected positions are full-time jobs. Other positions are more like part-time jobs. Government positions can last several years. Leaders work with other elected officials. They make plans and goals for the country.

Most state government meetings are open to the public. This is because many states have open meetings laws. These laws allow people to attend government meetings where issues that affect them are discussed. Citizens can see how decisions are made. The Freedom of Information Act also helps keep citizens informed.

It gives citizens the right to look at some government records. This helps people see if the government is serving them fairly. Each state has laws about requesting public documents. Citizens can ask to see documents such as papers, videos, computer records, and more.

THE POWER OF ONE CITIZEN

Lilly Ledbetter worked for the Goodyear Tire Company. She was paid less than men who did the same job. Ledbetter took her case to court and won. But in 2007, the Supreme Court overturned the decision. Ledbetter kept fighting for equal pay. In 2009, the Lilly Ledbetter Fair Pay Act was passed. It requires companies to pay workers fairly, no matter their age, gender, or race.

4

THE FUTURE OF DEMOCRACY

In the United States, every citizen can make change. The government depends on people's participation. Today, technology helps more people get involved. Even people too young to vote are speaking up. Change can happen when people work for it.

TECHNOLOGY

Computers, cell phones, and the internet have changed how people share information. It is now easier to get involved in democracy. Government news is available online. People can watch leaders speak and debate. Candidates running for

When Barack Obama ran for president, he used social media to connect with voters.

office can use social media to reach out to voters. Barack Obama ran for president in 2008. He used social media to reach thousands of people.

Technology also makes it easier to register to vote. In some states, people use computers to register online. Protesting is also easier with technology. Protests can be organized quickly using smartphones and social media. In 2020, teens planned a protest in Katy, Texas. They wanted to protest the killing of George Floyd. He was a Black man who was wrongfully killed by police in Minneapolis, Minnesota. The teens gathered hundreds of people together. They organized the protest in just four days.

EVERY VOICE MATTERS

There are many ways for people to get involved in democracy. Even people too young to vote can participate. Young people can help others register to vote. In many states, people ages sixteen and seventeen can work at the polls.

ROCK THE VOTE

In 1990, record producer Jeff Ayeroff started Rock the Vote. He wanted to help young people exercise their right to vote. The organization educates young people about voting. Its mission is to help them make their voices heard.

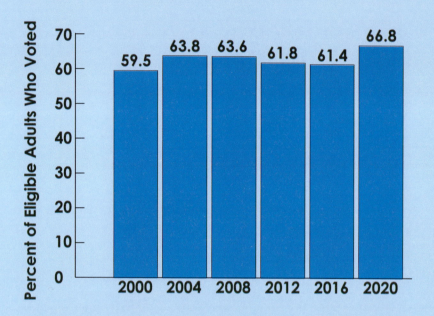

Source: Jacob Fabina, "Despite Pandemic Challenges, 2020 Election Had the Largest Increase in Voting Between Presidential Elections on Record," United States Census Bureau, April 29, 2021. www.census.gov.

Since the early 2000s, the percentage of people who vote in presidential elections has grown.

Young people can also volunteer to help candidates get elected. They can make phone calls or pass out information to inform voters about candidates. They can also use social media to share stories they care about.

Many young people are making a difference. Some educate others about important issues. Swedish climate activist Greta Thunberg started speaking up at age fifteen. She helps people understand how Earth's climate is changing. She inspires young people to vote on climate issues. She tells young people, "We can no longer let the people in power decide what is politically possible."[8]

The student-led March for Our Lives protests inspired many young people to vote.

Another group of teens organized a march in 2018. They were students from Marjory Stoneman Douglas High School in Florida. A student used a gun to kill other students at their school. The teens wanted to protest gun violence. They called their protest March for Our Lives. The protesters demanded stricter gun laws. They toured the country and registered 800,000 new voters. They inspired many young people to vote in the 2018 elections.

VOTING CHALLENGES TODAY

Voting should be easy for everyone. But some state laws have made voting harder. In Georgia, some people in lower-income communities must wait in long lines at the polls. Sometimes they wait for hours. This is because there are fewer polling locations in their communities. In 2021, Georgia passed a new law. It said food and water could not be handed out within 150 feet (46 m) of polling places. This makes it hard for older voters and people with disabilities to wait in long lines.

In 2023, thirty-five states had laws requiring voters to show an **identification** card, or ID. Eight states require photo IDs. Voters must show a driver's license or government ID. But over 21 million citizens do not have IDs. Some people support voter ID laws. An ID is proof that a voter is who he says he is. IDs reduce the number of people who vote unlawfully. But others

Long lines at polling places can make it harder for some people to vote.

think requiring IDs is unfair. Some voters cannot afford IDs. Others live far away from places where IDs are sold.

Another issue is access to polling places. Some voters cannot get off work in time to vote. Others must travel long distances to

In some states, voters are required to show a photo ID such as a driver's license or passport.

reach polling places. Some Native American voters live on reservations. They may have to travel long distances to reach the nearest polling place. In 2017, North Dakota passed a law requiring voters to have street addresses. Many Native Americans on reservations do not have street addresses. So their voting applications were rejected.

Democracy does not work unless all citizens take part. New problems arise every day. But when people are unhappy, there are ways to make change. Citizens can vote and protest. They can support new candidates or run for office themselves.

George H. W. Bush was the forty-first president. In a 1991 speech, he said, "Since the birth of our nation, 'we the people' has been the source of our strength."[9] Citizens must keep participating for democracy to succeed.

GLOSSARY

amendments
corrections or changes to a law or document

ballot
a sheet of paper or electronic form used to cast a vote

candidates
people who want to be considered for a government office

citizen
a person legally recognized as being part of a country

election
a process in which voters select government officials

federal
relating to a national government

identification
proof of a person's identity

polls
places where votes are recorded

ratified
formally approved

suffragists
people who fight for the right to vote

SOURCE NOTES

INTRODUCTION: YOUR VOTE IS YOUR VOICE

1. Quoted in Rebecca Chavoya, "Iris Galvan," *University of Texas at Austin Voces Oral History Center*, March 23, 2014. https://voces.lib.utexas.edu.

2. Quoted in Chavoya, "Iris Galvan."

CHAPTER ONE: THE ORIGINS OF US DEMOCRACY

3. "From Thomas Jefferson to Edward Tiffin, 2 February 1807," *Founders Online: National Archives*, n.d. https://founders.archives.gov.

4. "The Constitution of the United States," *National Archives*, February 3, 2023. www.archives.gov.

5. "President George Washington's First Inaugural Speech (1789)," *National Archives*, August 30, 2022. www.archives.gov.

CHAPTER TWO: THE ROLE OF CITIZENS

6. Quoted in Tanya Somanader, "President Obama on the Significance of a Civil Society," *White House: President Barack Obama*, September 23, 2014. https://obamawhitehouse.archives.gov.

CHAPTER THREE: PARTICIPATING IN GOVERNMENT

7. "Remarks by President Biden on Standing Up for Democracy," *White House*, November 3, 2022. www.whitehouse.gov.

CHAPTER FOUR: THE FUTURE OF DEMOCRACY

8. Quoted in Damian Carrington, "'Blah, Blah, Blah': Greta Thunberg Lambasts Leaders over Climate Crisis," *Guardian*, September 28, 2021. www.theguardian.com.

9. "Transcript of President's State of the Union Message to Nation," *New York Times*, January 30, 1991. www.nytimes.com.

FOR FURTHER RESEARCH

BOOKS

Jeff Foster, *For Which We Stand: How Our Government Works and Why It Matters*. New York: Scholastic, 2020.

Evan Sargent and Aura Lewis, *We the People: The United States Constitution Explored and Explained*. Beverly, MA: Quarto Publishing, 2020.

Shannon Weber, *Basher Civics: Democracy Rules!* New York: Kingfisher, 2020.

INTERNET SOURCES

Mina Fedor, "8 Questions for Elizabeth Clay Roy," *Time For Kids*, October 19, 2022. www.timeforkids.com.

Anna Starecheski and Laura Anastasia, "Should Teens Be Allowed to Vote?" *Scholastic*, August 2020. https://classroommagazines.scholastic.com

"Ten Ways Kids Too Young to Vote Can Get Involved in Politics," *YEA Camp*, n.d. https://yeacamp.org.

WEBSITES

Annenberg Classroom
www.annenbergclassroom.org

Annenberg Classroom provides videos, games, and timelines on constitutional concepts.

Kids in the House
https://kids-clerk.house.gov

Kids in the House has information for kids on the US House of Representatives. This is the legislative branch of the US government.

United States Courts
www.uscourts.gov

The official site of the US Courts provides information about the judicial branch, current judges, past court cases, and more.

INDEX

American Civil War, 32–33, 37

Biden, Joe, 29
Bill of Rights, 24

candidates, 7, 9–10, 22, 27, 42–43, 47–48, 50–51, 57
citizens, 8–9, 10–11, 13, 19, 20–21, 22–27, 28, 30, 34–35, 37, 39–40, 43–45, 46, 54, 57

Declaration of Independence, 17–18

elected officials, 13, 28, 44
elections, 9, 22–24, 37, 50, 53
executive branch, 19, 43

Fifteenth Amendment, 34–35, 39
Fourteenth Amendment, 34

Galvan, Iris, 6–10
Gettysburg Address, 32
grandfather clauses, 36–37

Jefferson, Thomas, 18
Johnson, Lyndon, 41
judicial branch, 19, 45

Ledbetter, Lilly, 45
legislative branch, 19, 21, 42–43
Lincoln, Abraham, 32

March for Our Lives, 52–53
Mayflower Compact, 14

National American Woman Suffrage Association (NAWSA), 37–38
National Woman Suffrage Association (NWSA), 37–38
Nineteenth Amendment, 39

open meetings laws, 44

Pilgrims, 14
poll taxes, 35
polling places, 9, 40, 49, 53–54, 55–56
presidents, 19, 21, 24, 27, 29, 32, 38, 41, 43, 48, 57

Revolutionary War, 17, 21

slavery, 30–33

Thunberg, Greta, 51

US Constitution, 10–11, 18, 19–21, 23, 24, 30, 34

voter IDs, 54-55
voting, 6-7, 9–11, 13, 22–24, 26, 28–30, 33–41, 46, 48, 49, 50, 51, 53–57
Voting Rights Act, 40–41

Washington, George, 21, 24

62

IMAGE CREDITS

Cover: © SDI Productions/iStockphoto
5: © LPETTET/iStockphoto
7: © H. A. Besen/iStockphoto
8: © SDI Productions/iStockphoto
11: © Anthony Ricci/Shutterstock Images
13: © milosk50/Shutterstock Images
15: © Keith Lance/iStockphoto
16: © Keith Lance/iStockphoto
23: © Rob Crandall/Shutterstock Images
25: © Diego G Diaz/Shutterstock Images
29: © Michael Scott Milner/Shutterstock Images
31: © Everett Collection/Shutterstock Images
35: © Everett Collection/Shutterstock Images
36: © Everett Collection/Shutterstock Images
38: © Everett Collection/Shutterstock Images
41: © Marion S. Trikosko/Library of Congress
43: © Mark Reinstein/Shutterstock Images
47: © zodebala/iStockphoto
50: © Red Line Editorial
52: © Hayk_Shalunts/Shutterstock Images
55: © Trevor Bexon/Shutterstock Images
56: © Rob Crandall/Shutterstock Images

ABOUT THE AUTHOR

Janie Havemeyer is the author of many books for young readers. Janie has a master's degree in education and has taught in schools. She lives in San Francisco, California. She voted in her first election when she was a college student.